PRINCE PHAAHLE

The winner's mindset

Mind over matter. The winners edge

First edition

Proofreading by Tshireparadise
Editing by Prince Phaahle
Typesetting by TPP

This book was professionally typeset on Reedsy.
Find out more at reedsy.com

Contents

1	Introduction	1
2	Chapter1(The power of mindset)	3
3	Chapter2(identifying and challenging limiting beliefs)	5
4	Chapter3(Building unshakable confidence)	8
5	Chapter 4(Cultivating resilience)	12
6	Chapter 5(Unleashing your inner brilliant)	14
7	Chapter 6(Sustaining success)	18
8	Chapter 7(Leaving a lasting legacy)	22
9	Chapter 8(Sustaining momentum)	26
10	Chapter 9(Leaving a lasting impact)	33
11	Chapter 10(Sustaining success)	38
12	Chapter 11(Beyond success:leaving a lasting legacy)	43
13	Chapter 12(Sustaining greatness:The journey continues)	47
14	Chapter 13(Unleashing your inner champion: The secret to...	50
15	Chapter 14(Maintaining momentum:overcoming obstacles and...	55
16	Chapter 15(Leaving a lasting legacy: The ultimate measure of...	59
17	Recap	62
18	Call to action	65

19 Inspirational note   68
20 Final thoughts   72
21 About the author   74
22 Final message   76

1

Introduction

Welcome to The Winner's Mindset, your guide to unlocking the secrets of success and achieving greatness. Do you ever wonder what sets apart the achievers from the dreamers? What drives Olympic champions, business moguls, and thought leaders to reach new heights? The answer lies not in their talent or luck, but in their mindset.

A winner's mindset is more than just a positive attitude; it's a powerful tool that empowers you to overcome obstacles, build resilience, and unlock your full potential. It's the ability to stay focused, motivated, and committed to your goals, even when the journey gets tough.

In the following pages, we'll explore the essential principles, strategies, and techniques required to cultivate a winner's mindset. You'll discover how to:
- ReWire your thoughts for success
- Build unshakeable confidence
- Develop a growth mindset
- Overcome fear, doubt, and self-limiting beliefs

- Stay motivated and focused on your goals

Through inspiring stories, practical exercises, and proven techniques, this book will equip you with the mental toughness and winning strategies necessary to achieve success in all areas of your life.

Get ready to unlock your inner winner and unleash your full potential. The journey starts now."

2

Chapter1(The power of mindset)

The greatest battle you'll ever fight is the one between your ears. Your mindset is the single most powerful tool you possess, shaping your perceptions, influencing your decisions, and determining your destiny. It's the spark that ignites your passions or the anchor that holds you back. Yet, for many of us, our mindset remains an untapped resource, a hidden force that drives our actions and reactions without our conscious awareness. In this chapter, we'll explore the transformative power of mindset, exposing the limiting beliefs that hold you back and introducing the core principles of a winner's mindset – a mindset that will revolutionize your approach to success, failure, and everything in between.Your mindset is the lens through which you view the world, filtering every experience, every conversation, and every opportunity. It's the internal compass that guides your decisions, influencing whether you see obstacles as insurmountable barriers or stepping stones to greatness. A winner's mindset doesn't just happen overnight; it's cultivated through intentional choices, disciplined habits, and a deep understanding of the thoughts, emotions, and beliefs that drive your actions. By recognizing and reframing your limiting thoughts, you'll unlock the potential to rewrite your story, reframe your failures, and redefine what's possible – setting the stage for a life of purpose, passion, and unparalleled success."

3

Chapter2(identifying and challenging limiting beliefs)

The Invisible Barriers to Success

"The greatest enemy of success is not failure, but the fear of failure. And that fear is often rooted in limiting beliefs – deeply ingrained thoughts and assumptions that hold you back from achieving your full potential. In this chapter, we'll explore the invisible barriers that keep you stuck, and provide practical strategies for challenging and overcoming them."

Section 1: Recognizing Limiting Beliefs

"Limiting beliefs can be subtle, masquerading as rational thoughts or self-protective instincts. But they can also be debilitating, stifling your creativity, confidence, and momentum. Common limiting beliefs include:

- I'm not good enough.
  - I'll never succeed.

- I'm too old/young.
- I don't have the right connections.
- I'm not smart/talented enough.

Take a moment to reflect on your own thoughts. What limiting beliefs might be holding you back?"

Section 2: Challenging Limiting Beliefs

"To overcome limiting beliefs, you must first acknowledge and challenge them. Ask yourself:

- Is this thought really true?
    - Is there evidence to support it?
    - Would I say this to a friend?
    - What would happen if I let go of this belief?

By questioning your limiting beliefs, you'll begin to dismantle the mental barriers that have held you back for too long."

Section 3: Replacing Limiting Beliefs

"Once you've identified and challenged your limiting beliefs, it's time to replace them with empowering ones. Consider:

- I am capable and competent.
    - I trust myself and my abilities.
    - I am worthy of success and happiness.
    - I can learn and grow.
    - I am resilient and adaptable.

Repeat these affirmations daily, and watch your mindset begin to shift."

Write down 3 limiting beliefs that hold you back and by doing that that's were a lot of things will start to change

"Today marks the dawn of a new era – the era of unapologetic self-belief. It's time to shatter the glass ceiling of doubt and unleash the unstoppable force within you. Confidence is not a gift, but a choice. It's the cumulative effect of every courageous step, every triumphant victory, and every lesson learned from defeat. As you embark on this transformative journey, remember that your worth is not defined by external validation, but by the unrelenting passion and resilience that burns within. You are capable of achieving greatness, not in spite of your flaws, but because of them. Embrace your uniqueness, own your strengths, and let your confidence soar. The world is waiting for the unstoppable version of you – let it emerge."

"As confidence grows, so does your capacity for taking bold action. The hesitant voice of self-doubt fades into the background, replaced by the assertive tone of self-assurance. You begin to trust your instincts, trust your decisions, and trust the process. Every accomplishment fuels your momentum, every setback becomes a valuable lesson, and every challenge becomes an opportunity to prove your strength. With unshakeable confidence, you'll walk taller, speak clearer, and inspire others to do the same. Your presence will command attention, your voice will command respect, and your dreams will command reality. The question is, what will you do with this unparalleled power? Will you hide or will you shine?"

4

Chapter3(Building unshakable confidence)

The Foundation of Success

"Confidence is the cornerstone of achievement. It's the spark that ignites passion, fuels resilience, and drives success. Without it, even the most talented individuals can falter. With it, ordinary people can achieve extraordinary feats. In this chapter, we'll explore the essential strategies for building unshakable confidence – the kind that withstands adversity, rejects self-doubt, and propels you toward greatness."

Section 1: Identifying and Challenging Negative Self-Talk

"The most significant obstacle to confidence is often our own inner critic. Negative self-talk can sabotage even the most promising opportunities. To overcome this, you must:

1. Recognize your inner dialogue
2. Challenge debilitating thoughts
3. Replace them with empowering affirmations

Examples:

- Negative: "I'm not good enough."
    - Challenge: "Is this thought really true?"
    - Replacement: "I'm capable and competent."

Section 2: Embracing Self-Acceptance

"Self-acceptance is the precursor to confidence. It's embracing your strengths, weaknesses, and uniqueness. Practice:

1. Self-compassion
2. Self-forgiveness
3. Self-appreciation

Remember, your worth isn't defined by external validation, but by your inherent value as a person."

Section 3: Cultivating Positive Experiences

"Confidence grows through experiences of success, no matter how small.:

1. Set achievable goals
2. Celebrate victories
3. Learn from setbacks

Every accomplishment builds momentum, reinforcing your confidence and resilience."

Section 4: Surrounding Yourself with Support

"The people you surround yourself with can either bolster or erode your confidence.:

1. Seek mentors and role models
2. Build a supportive network
3. Distance yourself from negativity

Surround yourself with those who uplift and inspire you."

Action Steps:

1. Write down 3 negative self-statements and challenge them.
2. Practice self-acceptance through daily affirmations.
3. Set 3 achievable goals and celebrate your successes.
4. Identify 2 supportive relationships to nurture.

"As confidence takes root, you'll notice a profound shift in your demeanor, from hesitant to assertive, from uncertain to decisive. Your body language will change, your tone will strengthen, and your words will carry weight. People will begin to notice the difference, too - they'll respect your boundaries, value your opinions, and seek your guidance. But remember, confidence is not a destination; it's a continuous journey. It requires nurturing, reinforcement, and intentional practice. Every day, you'll face choices: to assert yourself or shrink back, to trust yourself or doubt. Choose confidence, and watch your life transform into a masterpiece of purpose, passion, and unapologetic self-expression."

"Your confidence is not a reflection of your circumstances, but a reflection of your conviction. It's the unwavering faith in your abilities, your values, and your vision. When you stand tall in the midst of turmoil, when you speak truth to power, and when you refuse to compromise on your dreams, that's when the universe takes notice. That's when the doors of opportunity swing open, and the world begins to conspire in your favor. So don't wait for the perfect storm to gather confidence; create the storm yourself. Let your unwavering self-belief be the driving force that shatters obstacles, silences doubters, and unleashes the unstoppable version of you."

"Confidence isn't an absence of fear; it's a defiance of fear. It's the willingness to confront the unknown, to challenge the status quo, and to push beyond the boundaries of what's considered possible. When you embody this unyielding confidence, you'll inspire others to do the same. Your presence will become a catalyst for transformation, a reminder that greatness lies within reach. Don't let the doubts of others dictate your trajectory. You be the architect of your destiny, the captain of your soul. Build your foundation on the rock-solid conviction that you are capable, you are strong, and you are unstoppable."

5

Chapter 4(Cultivating resilience)

Resilience is the unsung hero of success, the quiet strength that separates champions from contenders. It's the ability to bounce back from adversity, to adapt in the face of uncertainty, and to emerge stronger and wiser. When you cultivate resilience, you're not just surviving – you're thriving. You're transforming obstacles into opportunities, setbacks into stepping stones, and failures into valuable lessons.The greatest myth about resilience is that it's innate, reserved for the select few who are born with an unbreakable spirit. But resilience is not a gift; it's a skill that can be developed, honed, and strengthened. It begins with a mindset shift, a conscious decision to view challenges as opportunities for growth rather than threats to your ego. When you adopt this mindset, you'll start to see the world differently – as a place of possibility, not limitation.Resilience is not about being impervious to pain or immune to fear. It's about facing your doubts, acknowledging your vulnerabilities, and pushing forward with courage and determination. It's about recognizing that every setback contains a hidden lesson, every failure a seed of future success. When you embody this resilience, you'll inspire others to do the same – to stand tall in the face of adversity, to fight for their dreams, and to emerge victorious.As you rise from the ashes of adversity, remember that every scar tells a story of strength, every struggle a testament to your unyielding spirit. You are not defined by your failures, but by your refusal to surrender. You are not weakened by your wounds, but made stronger by the courage to face them. So don't let the shadows of doubt creep in, don't let the whispers of fear hold you back. Instead, let your resilience be the beacon that illuminates your path, guiding you toward greatness. You are unstoppable, unbreakable, and unbeatable. Believe it, and the universe will conspire to make it so." "Life's greatest triumphs often lie just beyond the threshold of your comfort zone. It's in the unknown, the uncharted, and the uncomfortable that you'll discover your inner strength, your hidden potential, and your unshakeable resilience. So don't be afraid to venture into the darkness, for it's there that you'll find the spark that ignites your soul. Embrace the uncertainty, confront your fears, and push past the limits of what you thought was possible. For on the other side of fear lies freedom, on the other side of doubt lies discovery, and on the other side of adversity lies unparalleled growth.Your journey is unique, your struggles are real, and your victories are worthy of celebration. Don't compare your progress to others; compare it to the person you were yesterday. Every step forward, no matter how small, is a testament to your unwavering determination. Every obstacle overcome is a badge of honor, every lesson learned a valuable gem. You are not just building resilience; you are crafting a legacy of strength, a monument of courage, and a life of unapologetic purpose. Own your story, embrace your scars, and let your resilience be the guiding light that illuminates the path for others to follow."

6

Chapter 5(Unleashing your inner brilliant)

The greatest barrier to achieving greatness is often self-imposed. We doubt our abilities, question our worth, and settle for mediocrity. But what if you could silence the inner critic, shatter the glass ceiling of limitations, and unleash your full potential? What if you could tap into the inner greatness that lies within you, waiting to be unleashed? The truth is, you can.Your inner greatness is not a distant dream; it's a present reality waiting to be awakened. It's the spark that drives innovation, fuels creativity, and propels progress. It's the fire that burns within, urging you to push beyond the ordinary and achieve the extraordinary. To unleash this greatness, you must first recognize its presence, then nurture its growth, and finally, share its brilliance with the world.The journey to inner greatness begins with self-awareness – understanding your strengths, weaknesses, values, and passions. It requires embracing your uniqueness, celebrating your quirks, and leveraging your talents. When you know yourself, you'll discover the hidden reserves of potential, the untapped wellsprings of creativity, and the unbridled energy that drives achievement.As you unlock your inner greatness, you'll experience a profound shift in perspective. You'll see challenges as opportunities, obstacles as stepping stones, and setbacks as catalysts for growth. You'll develop an unshakeable confidence, an unwavering resilience, and an unrelenting drive to succeed. And when you share your greatness with the world, you'll inspire others to do the same, creating a ripple effect of excellence that transforms lives.Inner greatness is not solely reserved for the select few; it's a universal birthright. Every person has a unique contribution to make, a distinct impact to leave, and a lasting legacy to build. When you unleash your inner greatness, you'll join the ranks of those who have dared to defy convention, push past limitations, and achieve the impossible.

The greatest tragedy is not failing to reach your full potential but failing to recognize it in the first place. Don't let fear, doubt, or mediocrity hold you back. You have a unique gift, a singular perspective, and a powerful voice. Share it with the world, and watch as the landscape of possibility shifts to accommodate your greatness.Unleashing your inner greatness requires courage, conviction, and consistency. It demands that you show up fully, authentically, and unapologetically. You must be willing to take risks, challenge the status quo, and disrupt the norms. But the reward is worth it: a life of purpose, passion, and unparalleled fulfillment.As you embark on this journey, remember that greatness is not a destination; it's a process. It's the daily commitment to excellence, the relentless pursuit of growth, and the unwavering dedication to your vision. You are capable of achieving greatness, not in spite of your flaws but because of them.

The moment you decide to unleash your inner greatness, the universe conspires to support you. Opportunities emerge, doors open, and synchronicities align. But it's not magic — it's the natural consequence of aligning your actions, thoughts, and intentions with your highest potential.Your inner greatness is a beacon, shining brightly for all to see. It inspires others, motivates them, and challenges them to do the same. When you embody greatness, you become a catalyst for transformation, a spark that ignites a chain reaction of excellence.The greatest leaders, innovators, and changemakers didn't just achieve greatness — they inspired others to join them. They created movements, built communities, and left lasting legacies. You too can leave an indelible mark on the world, but it begins with embracing your own inner greatness.Unleashing your inner greatness requires vulnerability, transparency, and authenticity. It demands that you shed the masks, drop the pretenses, and reveal your true self. When you do, you'll discover that your uniqueness is your strength, your quirks are your advantages, and your vulnerabilities are your superpowers.As you walk the path of greatness, remember that it's not about achieving perfection; it's about embracing progress. It's not about being better than others; it's about being better than you were yesterday. Every step forward, every leap of faith, and every act of courage brings you closer to realizing your full potential.

Your inner greatness is a flame that flickers brightly, waiting to illuminate the world. Don't let fear, self-doubt, or external validation dim its light. You are the guardian of your own greatness, the curator of your own destiny. Protect it, nurture it, and share it with the world.The journey to greatness is not a solo endeavor; it's a symphony of collaboration, connection, and community. Surround yourself with people who amplify your strengths, challenge your weaknesses, and celebrate your successes. Together, you'll create a masterpiece of excellence.

Every achievement, every milestone, and every triumph is a testament to your inner greatness. Don't downplay your successes or diminish your accomplishments. Own them, celebrate them, and let them fuel your next level of growth.You are the architect of your own legacy, the author of your own story. Write a narrative of greatness, one that inspires generations to come. Your impact, influence, and inspiration will outlast you, leaving an indelible mark on the world.The world needs your greatness now more than ever. Don't hide, don't hesitate, and don't apologize for your brilliance. Unleash it, share it, and watch as the world transforms around you. Your greatness is the solution to someone's problem, the answer to someone's prayer.

7

Chapter 6(Sustaining success)

Success is not a destination; it's a journey of continuous growth, improvement, and evolution. To sustain success, you must adopt a mindset of perpetual progress, embracing challenges as opportunities to refine your skills, expand your knowledge, and deepen your impact.The greatest threat to success is complacency – the enemy of excellence. When you're at the top of your game, it's easy to become comfortable, relaxed, and stagnant. But comfort zones are danger zones, where growth goes to die. Stay hungry, stay humble, and stay focused on the next level.Sustaining success requires intentional effort, strategic planning, and disciplined execution. Set new goals, create accountability systems, and surround yourself with people who push you to excel. Celebrate milestones, but don't rest on laurels – instead, use them as stepping stones to greater heights.

The pursuit of excellence is a lifelong journey, not a short-term sprint. It demands resilience, adaptability, and creativity. Stay curious, stay open-minded, and stay willing to pivot when circumstances change. Your ability to adjust will become your greatest asset.To sustain success, you must also prioritize self-care – nurturing your physical, emotional, and mental well-being. Burnout, exhaustion, and depletion are major obstacles to maintaining momentum. Invest in your health, cultivate meaningful relationships, and prioritize activities that bring joy and balance.As you continue on the path of success, remember that true fulfillment lies in the journey, not the destination. Focus on the process, not just the outcome. Measure success not just by achievements, but by the positive impact you have on others, the growth you experience, and the legacy you build.

The sustainability of success depends on your ability to reinvent and innovate. Stay ahead of the curve by embracing new technologies, trends, and ideas. Invest in continuous learning, attend seminars, read books, and seek mentorship. The moment you stop learning is the moment you start stagnating.Your network is a critical component of sustaining success. Surround yourself with people who inspire, motivate, and challenge you. Build relationships with fellow achievers, thought leaders, and innovators. Collaborate, share knowledge, and support each other's growth.Resilience is key to sustaining success. Develop coping mechanisms to handle setbacks, failures, and criticism. Learn from mistakes, and use them as opportunities for growth. Celebrate your wins, but don't be defined by your losses.To sustain success, you must also lead with purpose and values. Stay true to your vision, mission, and principles. Make decisions that align with your core values, and prioritize integrity over expediency.

Sustaining success requires a growth mindset, a willingness to take calculated risks, and an ability to navigate uncertainty. Stay adaptable, stay agile, and stay open to new opportunities.Legacy thinking is essential to sustaining success. Consider the impact you want to leave on the world, the difference you want to make, and the values you want to instill. Build a legacy that transcends your achievements, one that inspires future generations.Your success is not solely yours; it's a collective achievement. Acknowledge the support of loved ones, mentors, and colleagues. Share your success, empower others, and create a ripple effect of excellence.

Sustaining success demands intentional reflection and self-awareness. Regularly assess your progress, adjust your strategies, and refine your vision. Identify blind spots, confront weaknesses, and leverage strengths.Your success is a platform for impact. Use it to uplift others, inspire change, and drive positive transformation. Share your story, mentor others, and create opportunities for growth.Legacy is not just about what you leave behind; it's about what you build into others. Invest in people, nurture relationships, and empower leaders. Your greatest legacy may be the leaders you develop.

To sustain success, cultivate a culture of gratitude and appreciation. Recognize the contributions of others, celebrate milestones, and express thanks.Sustaining success requires embracing change and uncertainty. Stay nimble, adapt quickly, and innovate continuously. View disruption as opportunity, not obstacle.Your success is not a solo act; it's a symphony of collaboration. Build strategic partnerships, forge meaningful connections, and leverage collective genius.The true measure of success lies in its durability, not just its intensity. Build foundations that last, create systems that sustain, and cultivate relationships that endure.Sustaining success is a marathon, not a sprint. Pace yourself, stay focused, and maintain momentum. Celebrate progress, learn from setbacks, and keep moving forward.

Sustaining success requires a mindset shift from scarcity to abundance. Believe that there's enough for everyone, and that your success creates opportunities for others.Your success is a catalyst for social responsibility. Use your platform to drive positive change, advocate for justice, and promote equality.Legacy thinking is about building timeless institutions, not temporary monuments. Focus on creating sustainable systems, not fleeting fame.To sustain success, prioritize authenticity over image. Stay true to yourself, your values, and your mission.

The sustainability of success depends on your ability to inspire and empower others. Develop leaders, mentor talent, and create a culture of excellence.Your success is not just about achieving goals; it's about becoming the best version of yourself. Cultivate self-awareness, emotional intelligence, and spiritual depth.Sustaining success requires embracing vulnerability and imperfection. Admit weaknesses, ask for help, and learn from failures.The true test of success lies in its transferability. Can others replicate your results? Can your success be scaled?Sustaining success demands a long-term perspective. Focus on decades, not days; legacy, not luck.

8

Chapter 7(Leaving a lasting legacy)

As you stand at the pinnacle of success, you're faced with a new challenge: leaving a lasting legacy. Your impact, influence, and achievements have paved the way for others to follow. Now, it's time to cement your legacy.A lasting legacy is built on the foundation of purpose, passion, and perseverance. It's the culmination of a life dedicated to making a difference, pushing boundaries, and inspiring others.Your legacy is not just about what you achieve; it's about who you become. It's the person you've grown into, the values you've upheld, and the principles you've lived by.To leave a lasting legacy, focus on building institutions, not monuments. Create systems that sustain, processes that endure, and cultures that thrive.

Legacy thinking requires a shift from individual achievement to collective impact. Invest in others, empower leaders, and create opportunities for growth.Your legacy is a reflection of your values, priorities, and character. Ensure that it reflects your true self, your passions, and your purpose.A lasting legacy transcends time, trends, and circumstances. It's built on timeless principles, universal values, and enduring relationships.As you contemplate your legacy, ask yourself: What will outlast me? What will inspire future generations? What will leave an indelible mark on the world?

Legacy is not solely reserved for the famous or influential. Every person has the potential to leave a lasting impact, regardless of their background or circumstances. Your legacy is a reflection of your unique experiences, skills, and passions.As you build your legacy, focus on the ripple effect. How will your actions, decisions, and achievements impact others? Will you inspire, educate, or empower? Will you leave a trail of positivity, kindness, and compassion?Your legacy is a story waiting to be written. Every chapter, every verse, and every sentence is a testament to your resilience, determination, and character. Write a narrative that inspires, motivates, and uplifts.Legacy thinking requires patience, persistence, and perspective. It's a long-term investment in the future, a bet on the potential of others, and a trust in the power of collective impact.The greatest legacies are built on the foundation of relationships. Nurture connections, foster community, and prioritize people. Your legacy will be measured by the lives you've touched, the hearts you've healed, and the minds you've inspired.

A lasting legacy is not just about what you leave behind; it's about what you leave within others. Deposit wisdom, kindness, and love into the lives of those around you.Your legacy is a reflection of your values, priorities, and choices. Align your actions with your purpose, your passions with your principles.Legacy is not an endpoint; it's a continuum. It's a chain of events, a series of decisions, and a collection of moments that define your impact.The true measure of legacy lies in its sustainability, not just its visibility. Build systems, create processes, and establish cultures that endure.

A lasting legacy requires intentional effort, strategic planning, and disciplined execution. It's a marathon, not a sprint; a journey, not a destination.Your legacy is shaped by your daily choices, habits, and actions. Make decisions that align with your purpose, prioritize relationships, and cultivate character.

Legacy thinking demands a willingness to let go of control and trust in the potential of others. Empower leaders, mentor talent, and create opportunities for growth.The greatest legacies transcend generations, industries, and geography. They inspire movements, spark innovations, and leave an indelible mark on humanity.Your legacy is a testament to your resilience, adaptability, and creativity. Share your story, teach your lessons, and inspire others to persevere.A lasting legacy is built on authenticity, integrity, and vulnerability. Be true to yourself, admit weaknesses, and learn from failures.

Legacy is not solely about achievement; it's about impact. Measure success not just by milestones, but by the lives changed, hearts touched, and minds inspired.Your legacy will outlast your lifetime. Consider how you want to be remembered, what values you want to instill, and what difference you want to make.To build a lasting legacy, focus on the intersection of passion, purpose, and proficiency. Leverage your strengths, pursue your passions, and make a meaningful impact.The power of legacy lies in its ability to inspire, motivate, and transform. Leave a legacy that ignites a fire within others, fuels their passions, and empowers their pursuit of excellence.

Legacy is a bridge connecting the past to the future. It honors the sacrifices of those who came before while inspiring generations to come.Your legacy is a reflection of your values, priorities, and character. Ensure it aligns with your true self and inspires others to do the same.Building a lasting legacy requires perseverance, grit, and determination. Overcome obstacles, push through challenges, and stay focused on your vision.

A strong legacy fosters a culture of excellence, innovation, and collaboration. Empower others to strive for greatness and create a ripple effect of success.Legacy thinking demands a global perspective, considering the impact of your actions on diverse communities and future generations.Your legacy will be shaped by the relationships you nurture. Invest in people, foster meaningful connections, and prioritize love and kindness.

A lasting legacy transcends personal achievement, focusing on the greater good. Strive to make a difference, leave a mark, and inspire positive change.To cement your legacy, document your journey, share your wisdom, and teach others. Leave a blueprint for success and a roadmap for impact.Your legacy is a testament to your faith, hope, and resilience. Share your story, inspire others, and demonstrate the power of the human spirit.Building a lasting legacy requires humility, gratitude, and forgiveness. Recognize the contributions of others, acknowledge your weaknesses, and let go of grudges.

9

Chapter 8(Sustaining momentum)

Sustaining momentum requires relentless drive, unwavering focus, and strategic planning. Stay committed to your vision, adapt to changing circumstances, and continuously improve.Momentum builders prioritize self-care, nurturing their physical, emotional, and mental well-being. Invest in activities that recharge your batteries, fuel your passions, and enhance your resilience.

To maintain momentum, surround yourself with positive influences, supportive networks, and inspiring role models. Foster relationships that uplift, motivate, and challenge you.Resilience is key to sustaining momentum. Develop coping mechanisms to navigate setbacks, reframe failures as learning opportunities, and celebrate small wins.Momentum-sustaining habits include setting realistic goals, tracking progress, and celebrating milestones. Stay accountable, focused, and motivated.Continuous ly seek knowledge, wisdom, and innovative strategies to stay ahead. Attend seminars, read books, and engage with thought leaders.

Embracing change and uncertainty is crucial for sustaining momentum. Stay adaptable, agile, and open to new opportuniti es.Effective time management and prioritization are essential for maintaining momentum. Focus on high-impact activities, delegate tasks, and eliminate distractions.To sustain momentum, lead with purpose, values, and integrity. Stay true to your mission, prioritize ethics, and inspire others.Momentum is contagious. Share your enthusiasm, inspire others, and create a ripple effect of success.

Sustaining momentum demands intentional effort to overcome complacency. Continuously challenge yourself, seek feedback, and push beyond comfort zones.Momentum builders prioritize accountability, seeking mentors, coaches, and peers who inspire growth. Surround yourself with people who expect excellence .Resilience is strengthened through adversity. View obstacles as opportunities to grow, learn, and improve.To maintain momentum, celebrate progress, not perfection. Acknowledge small wins, learn from setbacks, and stay focused on the journey.

Consistency breeds momentum. Establish routines, habits, and rituals that support your goals.Momentum-sustaining mindsets include curiosity, creativity, and openness. Stay receptive to new ideas, explore innovative solutions, and think outside the box.Effective momentum builders prioritize self-awareness, recognizing strengths, weaknesses, and areas for improvement.

Sustaining momentum requires embracing vulnerability, admitting weaknesses, and asking for help.Momentum is amplified through collaboration, partnership, and community. Build strategic alliances, foster meaningful connections, and leverage collective genius.To maintain momentum, stay flexible, adaptable, and responsive to changing circumstances.Mome ntum builders continuously seek inspiration, motivation, and encouragement.

Momentum is fueled by passion, purpose, and meaning. Connect with your why, ignite your enthusiasm, and pursue your passions.Sustaining momentum demands intentional effort to overcome fear, doubt, and uncertainty. Reframe negative self-talk, focus on strengths, and visualize success.Resilience is critical to maintaining momentum. Develop coping strategies, practice self-care, and prioritize well-being.Consistency is key to building momentum. Establish routines, set realistic goals, and track progress.Momentum-sustaining habits include continuous learning, self-reflection, and growth. Seek feedback, mentorship, and coaching.Effective momentum builders prioritize relationships, nurturing networks, and fostering community.

Sustaining momentum requires embracing change, adapting to challenges, and innovating solutions.Momentum is amplified through recognition, celebration, and gratitude. Acknowledge achievements, appreciate support, and express thanks.To maintain momentum, focus on progress, not perfection. Learn from setbacks, adjust strategies, and stay focused on the journey.Momentum builders continuously seek inspiration, motivation, and encouragement from within and outside.Sustaining momentum demands a growth mindset, openness to learning, and willingness to evolve.

Sustaining momentum requires embracing challenges as opportunities for growth. View obstacles as stepping stones to success.Momentum builders prioritize authenticity, staying true to themselves and their values. Integrity fuels resilience and perseverance.Continuous improvement is essential to maintaining momentum. Seek feedback, analyze performance, and adjust strategies.Resilience is strengthened through gratitude, positivity, and self-care. Nurture a supportive network, practice mindfulness, and prioritize well-being.

Momentum-sustaining habits include setting realistic goals, tracking progress, and celebrating milestones.Effective momentum builders leverage technology, tools, and resources to streamline processes and amplify impact.Sustaining momentum demands adaptability, agility, and openness to change. Stay flexible, responsive, and innovative.Momentum is amplified through collaboration, partnership, and strategic alliances. Foster meaningful connections, share knowledge, and leverage collective genius.

To maintain momentum, focus on the process, not just the outcome. Celebrate small wins, learn from setbacks, and stay focused on the journey.Momentum builders continuously seek inspiration, motivation, and encouragement from diverse sources.Sustaining momentum requires a forward-thinking mindset, envisioning the future, and planning for growth.Legacy thinking fuels momentum, considering the long-term impact of your actions.Momentum is a choice, requiring intentional effort, discipline, and commitment.

Momentum builders recognize that success is a journey, not a destination. They celebrate progress, learn from setbacks, and stay focused on the journey.Sustaining momentum demands a culture of continuous improvement. Encourage experimentation, learning from failures, and innovation.Resilience is critical to maintaining momentum. Develop coping strategies, prioritize self-care, and foster a supportive network.Effective momentum builders prioritize accountability, seeking mentors, coaches, and peers who inspire growth.Momentum-sustaining habits include setting realistic goals, tracking progress, and celebrating milestones.

To maintain momentum, focus on the why, not just the what. Connect with your purpose, passion, and values.Sustaining momentum requires embracing uncertainty, adapting to change, and innovating solutions.Momentum builders continuously seek knowledge, wisdom, and best practices.Legacy thinking fuels momentum, considering the long-term impact of your actions.Momentum is amplified through recognition, celebration, and gratitude.To sustain momentum, prioritize relationships, nurture networks, and foster community.Continuous learning and self-reflection are essential to maintaining momentum.Momentum builders stay humble, recognizing that success is a team effort.Sustaining momentum demands intentional effort, discipline, and commitment.

Momentum builders recognize that setbacks are temporary and opportunities for growth. They rebound with resilience and determination.Sustaining momentum requires clarity, focus, and prioritization. Eliminate distractions, streamline processes, and concentrate on high-impact activities.

Effective momentum builders cultivate a growth mindset, embracing challenges and viewing failures as learning experiences.To maintain momentum, celebrate milestones, acknowledge progress, and reward yourself.

Momentum-sustaining habits include continuous learning, self-reflection, and improvement.Resilience is strengthened through positive self-talk, affirmations, and visualization.Sustaining momentum demands adaptability, agility, and openness to change.

Momentum builders foster meaningful connections, collaborations, and strategic partnerships.Legacy thinking fuels momentum, considering the lasting impact of your achievements.To sustain momentum, prioritize self-care, well-being, and physical health.

Continuous improvement and innovation are essential to maintaining momentum.Momentum builders stay focused on the big picture, aligning daily actions with long-term vision.Sustaining momentum requires intentional effort, discipline, and commitment to excellence.Effective momentum builders recognize the power of community, leveraging collective genius and support.Momentum is amplified through recognition, gratitude, and celebration of others' successes.

Momentum builders recognize that success is a marathon, not a sprint. They pace themselves, conserve energy, and stay focused on the finish line.

Sustaining momentum demands resilience, grit, and determination. Bounce back from setbacks, learn from failures, and keep moving forward.

Effective momentum builders prioritize accountability, seeking mentors, coaches, and peers who inspire growth.To maintain momentum, stay flexible, adapt to change, and innovate solutions.

Momentum-sustaining habits include continuous learning, self-reflection, and improvement.Legacy thinking fuels momentum, considering the lasting impact of your achievements.

Momentum builders foster meaningful connections, collaborations, and strategic partnerships.Sustaining momentum requires intentional effort, discipline, and commitment to excellence.Effective momentum builders recognize the power of community, leveraging collective genius and support.

Momentum is amplified through recognition, gratitude, and celebration of others' successes.To sustain momentum, prioritize self-awareness, emotional intelligence, and mental toughness.Continuous improvement and innovation are essential to maintaining momentum.

Momentum builders stay focused on the big picture, aligning daily actions with long-term vision.Sustaining momentum demands a growth mindset, embracing challenges and viewing failures as learning experiences.Momentum builders continuously seek knowledge, wisdom, and best practices.

10

Chapter 9(Leaving a lasting impact)

Leaving a lasting impact requires a deliberate effort to make a difference in the lives of others.A lasting impact is built on a foundation of purpose, passion, and values.Effective impact-makers prioritize relationships, fostering meaningful connections and strategic partnerships.

To leave a lasting impact, focus on the legacy you want to leave, not just the achievements you want to attain.Impactful leaders inspire, motivate, and empower others to achieve their full potential.A lasting impact requires resilience, perseverance, and determination.

Continuous learning, self-reflection, and improvement are essential to leaving a lasting impact.Momentum builders recognize the power of community, leveraging collective genius and support.

Leaving a lasting impact demands intentional effort, discipline, and commitment to excellence.Effective impact-makers prioritize self-awareness, emotional intelligence, and mental toughness.A lasting impact is measured by the lives changed, hearts touched, and minds inspired.To leave a lasting impact, stay focused on the big picture, aligning daily actions with long-term vision.Sustaining momentum requires embracing challenges, adapting to change, and innovating solutions.Legacy thinking fuels impact, considering the lasting consequences of your actions.

A lasting impact requires a willingness to take risks, challenge the status quo, and innovate.Effective impact-makers prioritize authenticity, integrity, and transparency.To leave a lasting impact, focus on the process, not just the outcome.Impactful leaders empower others to take ownership, make decisions, and drive change.

A lasting impact is built on a foundation of strong relationships, trust, and communication.Continuous learning, self-reflection, and improvement are essential to leaving a lasting impact.Momentum builders recognize the power of storytelling, sharing their message and inspiring others.

Leaving a lasting impact demands resilience, grit, and determination.Effective impact-makers prioritize self-care, well-being, and physical health.A lasting impact requires a long-term perspective, considering the consequences of your actions.

To leave a lasting impact, stay humble, recognize the contributions of others, and celebrate their successes.Impactful leaders foster a culture of collaboration, inclusivity, and diversity.A lasting impact is measured by the positive change you create in the world.Effective impact-makers prioritize accountability, seeking feedback and continuously improving.Leaving a lasting impact requires intentional effort, discipline, and commitment to excellence.

Impactful leaders recognize the power of mentorship, guiding and supporting others.A lasting impact requires embracing failure as a learning opportunity.Effective impact-makers prioritize community engagement, giving back and making a difference.

To leave a lasting impact, focus on the greater good, putting others' needs before your own.Continuous learning and self-improvement are essential to leaving a lasting impact.Momentum builders recognize the power of networking, building meaningful connections.

Leaving a lasting impact demands authenticity, vulnerability, and transparency.Effective impact-makers prioritize relationships, nurturing and investing in people.A lasting impact requires a clear vision, aligning actions with purpose.

Impactful leaders inspire others to take action, mobilizing change.To leave a lasting impact, stay adaptable, responsive, and innovative.Effective impact-makers prioritize self-awareness, recognizing strengths and weaknesses.

A lasting impact is built on a foundation of integrity, ethics, and values.Momentum builders recognize the power of legacy, considering the long-term consequences.Leaving a lasting impact requires intentional effort, discipline, and commitment.Effective impact-makers prioritize gratitude, appreciation, and recognition.

Impactful leaders recognize the power of empowerment, unleashing others' potential.A lasting impact requires embracing diversity, inclusivity, and equity.Effective impact-makers prioritize storytelling, sharing experiences and inspiring others.To leave a lasting impact, focus on solutions, not problems.Continuous innovation and improvement are essential to leaving a lasting impact.

Momentum builders recognize the power of collaboration, partnering for success. A lasting impact demands resilience, perseverance, and determination.

Effective impact-makers prioritize feedback, seeking constructive criticism.A lasting impact requires a growth mindset, embracing challenges and learning.Impactful leaders foster a culture of excellence, striving for continuous improvement.

To leave a lasting impact, stay focused on the mission, aligning actions with purpose.Effective impact-makers prioritize relationships, building trust and credibility.A lasting impact is built on a foundation of accountability, transparency, and integrity.Momentum builders recognize the power of recognition, celebrating others' successes.

Leaving a lasting impact requires intentional effort, discipline, and commitment.Effective impact-makers prioritize legacy, considering the long-term consequences.Impactful leaders inspire others to make a difference, creating a ripple effect.

11

Chapter 10(Sustaining success)

Sustaining success requires ongoing effort, discipline, and commitment.Effective winners prioritize continuous learning, self-reflection, and improvement.To sustain success, focus on the process, not just the outcome.Winners recognize the power of habits, building routines that support their goals.

Sustaining success demands resilience, perseverance, and adaptability.Continuous innovation and improvement are essential to staying ahead.Winners prioritize relationships, nurturing networks and fostering collaboration.

To sustain success, stay humble, recognize the contributions of others, and celebrate their successes.Effective winners prioritize self-awareness, recognizing strengths and weaknesses.Sustaining success requires intentional effort, discipline, and commitment to excellence.

Winners recognize the power of legacy, considering the long-term consequences.Continuous growth and development are essential to sustaining success.

To sustain success, stay focused on the mission, aligning actions with purpose.Effective winners prioritize accountability, seeking feedback and continuously improving.Sustaining success demands a growth mindset, embracing challenges and learning.

Sustaining success requires embracing vulnerability, openness, and authenticity.Effective winners prioritize self-awareness, recognizing strengths, weaknesses, and emotions.

To sustain success, focus on the journey, not just the destination.Winners recognize the power of mindfulness, staying present and focused.Sustaining success demands resilience, grit, and determination.

Effective winners prioritize relationships, building trust and strong connections.To sustain success, stay adaptable, responsive, and innovative.Winners recognize the power of legacy, leaving a lasting impact.

Sustaining success requires intentional effort, discipline, and commitment.Effective winners prioritize gratitude, appreciation, and recognition.Continuous learning and growth are essential to sustaining success.

To sustain success, stay humble, recognizing the contributions of others.Effective winners prioritize accountability, seeking feedback and continuously improving.Sustaining success demands a growth mindset, embracing challenges and learning.Winners recognize the power of community, leveraging collective genius.

As you stand on the summit of success, remember that the journey is far from over. The true test of greatness lies in sustaining your achievements.Embracing challenges with courage and resilience is the hallmark of a true winner.Your legacy is not just about what you achieve, but how you inspire others to do the same.

The pursuit of excellence is a lifelong journey, and every step forward is a victory.Don't just celebrate your successes – use them as stepping stones to even greater heights.It's time to shift into high gear and take your success to the next level!You've worked hard to get here, now it's time to make it last.

Don't let complacency creep in – stay hungry, stay focused, and keep pushing forward.The only way to sustain success is to keep innovating, keep learning, and keep growing.You're not just building a legacy – you're creating a movement.

Remember, success is not a destination – it's a journey of growth and self-discovery.Every setback is an opportunity to learn and come back stronger.You are capable of achieving greatness, and sustaining it is within your reach.

Celebrate your wins, no matter how small, and use them as momentum to keep moving forward.Your success inspires others, so keep shining your light!Empowering Tone Take ownership of your success and recognize your worth.You have the power to create the legacy you desire – now go make it happen.

Sustaining success requires courage, resilience, and determination – and you have it all.Don't let anyone dull your sparkle – keep shining and inspiring others.Your success is a testament to your strength and perseverance.

Unlock your full potential and unleash a wave of success that transforms your life.Your legacy is a reflection of your values, passions, and commitment to excellence.

Sustaining success requires embracing challenges as opportunities for growth.You are the architect of your destiny; design a life of purpose and achievement.Every accomplishment is a stepping stone to greater heights; keep pushing forward.

As you soar to new heights, remember to stay grounded and humble.Success is not just about achieving goals; it's about becoming the best version of yourself.Your journey inspires others; share your story and ignite a movement.Don't just sustain success – amplify it by continuously learning and innovating.You are a beacon of hope and inspiration; shine brightly and shatter limitations.

It's time to turbocharge your success and blast through obstacles.Unleash your inner strength and resilience to overcome any challenge.Sustaining success requires a relentless pursuit of excellence.You're on a roll; keep the momentum going and crush your goals.Every victory is a catalyst for greater achievements; celebrate and keep striving.

Don't let success go to your head; stay focused and keep grinding.You've got this! Believe in yourself and your abilities.Sustaining success demands discipline, hard work, and determination.You're not just sustaining success – you're building a legacy.Stay hungry for greatness and continuously push the boundaries.

12

Chapter 11(Beyond success:leaving a lasting legacy)

As winners, we strive for success, but true fulfillment comes from leaving a lasting legacy.A legacy is more than achievements; it's the impact we have on others and the world.Effective winners prioritize building a legacy that transcends their own success.To leave a lasting legacy, focus on the value you bring to others, not just your own accomplishments.

Legacy thinking requires considering the long-term consequences of your actions.Winners recognize the power of mentorship, empowering others to carry on their legacy.Beyond success lies significance; strive to make a meaningful difference.To leave a lasting legacy, stay true to your values, passions, and purpose.Effective winners prioritize relationships, building a network of lasting connections.Legacy is built on a foundation of integrity, ethics, and social responsibility.

Your legacy is a reflection of your character, values, and passions. Own it.As you build a lasting legacy, remember that every life you touch is a ripple of impact.Don't just leave a legacy – create a movement that inspires generations.Your legacy is a testament to your resilience, determination, and heart.Unleash your inner leader and build a legacy that changes the game.Legacy is not just about what you achieve, but how you inspire others to achieve.

Take ownership of your legacy and make it a reflection of your greatness.You have the power to create a lasting impact; use it wisely.Every obstacle overcome is an opportunity to strengthen your legacy.Don't just build a legacy – ignite a revolution of success.Your legacy is a gift to the world; share it generously.Don't let fear hold you back – leave a legacy that makes history.You are the architect of your legacy; design it with purpose.

Your legacy is a reflection of your character, values, and passions. Own it. As you build a lasting legacy, remember that every life you touch is a ripple of impact. Don't just leave a legacy – create a movement that inspires generations. Your legacy is a testament to your resilience, determination, and heart.

Unleash your inner leader and build a legacy that changes the game. Legacy is not just about what you achieve, but how you inspire others to achieve. Take ownership of your legacy and make it a reflection of your greatness. You have the power to create a lasting impact; use it wisely.

Every obstacle overcome is an opportunity to strengthen your legacy. Don't just build a legacy – ignite a revolution of success. Your legacy is a gift to the world; share it generously. Don't let fear hold you back – leave a legacy that makes history.You are the architect of your legacy; design it with purpose. Build a legacy that transcends time and inspires future generations. Your legacy is a reflection of your values, passions, and commitment to excellence. Make it count.

Legacy is built on a foundation of integrity, ethics, and social responsibility. Effective winners prioritize relationships, building a network of lasting connections. To leave a lasting legacy, stay true to your values, passions, and purpose.

Beyond success lies significance; strive to make a meaningful difference. Winners recognize the power of mentorship, empowering others to carry on their legacy. Leave a legacy that inspires others to strive for greatness.

A lasting legacy requires dedication, perseverance, and resilience. It's the culmination of a life well-lived, with purpose and intention. Effective winners understand that legacy is not just about what they achieve, but how they inspire others to achieve. By building a lasting legacy, you create a ripple effect that impacts generations.

Your legacy is a reflection of your character, values, and passions. It's the story of your life, written in the hearts of those you've touched. Don't let fear or doubt hold you back from leaving a lasting impact. Embrace your uniqueness and share your gifts with the world. As you build your legacy, remember that every moment counts.

Legacy is not just about achieving greatness; it's about inspiring others to do the same. Winners recognize the power of mentorship, empowering others to carry on their legacy. By investing in others, you ensure that your legacy lives on. Leave a legacy that inspires others to strive for greatness, to push beyond their limits, and to achieve their dreams.

Building a lasting legacy requires intentional effort, discipline, and commitment. It's a marathon, not a sprint. Effective winners prioritize relationships, building a network of lasting connections. They understand that legacy is built on a foundation of integrity, ethics, and social responsibility.

Your legacy is your gift to the world. Share it generously, without expectation of reward or recognition. As you build your legacy, remember that every life you touch is a ripple of impact. Don't just leave a legacy – create a movement that inspires generations. Unleash your inner leader and build a legacy that changes the game.

Chapter 12(Sustaining greatness:The journey continues)

Sustaining greatness requires ongoing effort, discipline, and commitment. Winners recognize that success is a journey, not a destination. To stay on top, continuously improve, innovate, and push boundaries.

Effective winners prioritize self-reflection, seeking feedback and learning from failures. They recognize the power of resilience, bouncing back from setbacks and adversity. Sustaining greatness demands a growth mindset, embracing challenges and lifelong learning.

Winners understand the importance of relationships, nurturing networks and fostering collaboration. They prioritize self-care, maintaining physical and mental well-being. Sustaining greatness requires intentional effort, discipline, and commitment to excellence.

To sustain greatness, focus on the process, not just the outcome.

Celebrate milestones, but stay humble and hungry. Continuously seek knowledge, best practices, and innovative solutions. Winners recognize the power of legacy, considering the lasting impact of their actions.

Sustaining greatness is a choice, requiring deliberate action and dedication. Winners prioritize accountability, seeking feedback and continuously improving. They recognize the power of gratitude, appreciating the journey and its supporters.

Sustaining greatness requires embracing change and adapting to new challenges. Winners recognize the importance of staying relevant, innovative, and forward-thinking. Continuously seek knowledge, best practices, and cutting-edge solutions to stay ahead.

Effective winners prioritize self-awareness, recognizing strengths and weaknesses. They surround themselves with a supportive network, fostering collaboration and growth. Sustaining greatness demands resilience, perseverance, and determination.

To sustain greatness, focus on the big picture, aligning daily actions with long-term vision. Winners recognize the power of focus, eliminating distractions and staying committed. Continuously evaluate and adjust strategies to ensure alignment with goals.

Sustaining greatness requires intentional effort, discipline, and commitment to excellence. Winners prioritize accountability, seeking feedback and continuously improving. They recognize

the power of gratitude, appreciating the journey and its supporters.

Winners understand the importance of legacy, considering the
lasting impact of their actions. Sustaining greatness requires
leaving a lasting legacy, inspiring others to strive for greatness.
Continuously seek opportunities to make a meaningful difference.

Effective winners prioritize relationships, nurturing networks
and fostering collaboration. They recognize the power of mentorship, empowering others to achieve greatness. Sustaining
greatness demands investing in people and communities.Sustai
ning greatness requires embracing challenges as opportunities
for growth. Winners recognize the power of resilience, bouncing
back from setbacks and adversity. Continuously seek knowledge,
best practices, and innovative solutions to stay ahead.

Chapter 13(Unleashing your inner champion: The secret to unstoppable success)

This chapter reveals the ultimate secret to achieving unstoppable success: unleashing your inner champion. Every winner has an inner champion, a driving force that propels them to greatness. It's time to unlock yours.

The inner champion is the voice of confidence, resilience, and determination. It's the spark that ignites your passions and fuels your pursuits. To unleash your inner champion, you must first identify and silence your inner critic.

The inner critic is the voice of doubt, fear, and limitation. It's the obstacle that stands between you and greatness. Winners recognize the power of their inner critic and confront it head-on.

Unleashing your inner champion requires embracing your uniqueness and rejecting mediocrity. It demands courage, vulnerability, and a willingness to take risks. Winners understand that their inner champion is their greatest asset.

Unstoppable confidence
  Unwavering resilience
  Unrelenting determination
  Unbridled creativity
  Unmatched success

Join the ranks of winners who have unleashed their inner champion. Unlock your full potential and achieve unstoppable success.

Unleashing your inner champion requires embracing vulner-ability and authenticity. Winners recognize that vulnerability is strength, not weakness. By being true to themselves, they unlock their unique potential.

Your inner champion is your inner compass, guiding you toward greatness. Listen to its voice, and you'll discover your purpose, passion, and drive. Ignore it, and you'll settle for mediocrity.

The inner champion mindset is contagious. When you unleash yours, you inspire others to do the same. Together, you'll create a wave of unstoppable success.To sustain your inner champion, prioritize self-care and self-compassion. Nurture your mind, body, and spirit. Recognize that setbacks are opportunities for growth.

Effective winners celebrate their inner champion's victories, no matter how small. They acknowledge progress, not perfection.

By doing so, they reinforce their inner champion's voice.Unleashing your inner champion unlocks your creative potential. You'll innovate, take risks, and push boundaries. Your unique perspective will shape the world.

Your inner champion is your legacy. It's the impact you leave on others, the difference you make. Unleash it, and you'll leave an indelible mark.The inner champion journey is lifelong. It requires commitment, resilience, and determination. Winners understand that unleashing their inner champion is just the beginning.

As you unleash your inner champion, remember:
    You are unstoppable.
    You are unique.
    You are powerful.
    You are a winner.

Unleashing your inner champion transforms your relationships. You'll attract people who resonate with your authenticity and passion. Together, you'll create meaningful connections.Your inner champion fuels your purpose, driving you to make a lasting impact. Winners recognize their purpose is bigger than themselves. They serve, inspire, and leave a legacy.Embracing your inner champion requires courage, resilience, and determination. You'll face challenges, but your inner strength will propel you forward.

To unleash your inner champion, focus on identifying and overcoming self-limiting beliefs, cultivating self-awareness and emotional intelligence, developing a growth mindset and embracing challenges, surrounding yourself with positive influences, and embracing vulnerability and authenticity.Unleashing your inner champion unlocks unwavering confidence, unrelenting passion, unbridled creativity, unmatched resilience, and unstoppable success.Your inner champion is your greatest asset. Invest in it, nurture it, and unleash its full potential.

Winners understand that unleashing their inner champion is a lifelong journey. They commit to continuous growth, learning, and self-improvement.You are capable of achieving greatness. You are worthy of success and happiness. You are a force to be reckoned with. You are unstoppable.

Unleashing your inner champion ignites a fire within, propelling you toward greatness. It's the spark that sets your passions ablaze.Self-doubt and fear are conquered by your inner champion's unwavering confidence. You'll rise above obstacles.Your inner champion fuels your creativity, innovation, and problem-solving. It's the source of your unique perspective.Embracing your inner champion requires embracing your true self. Authenticity is the foundation of unstoppable success.

Your inner champion inspires others, leaving a lasting legacy. Your impact resonates beyond your lifetime.Unleashing your inner champion unlocks hidden potential. You'll achieve what you thought was impossible.Winners nurture their inner champion through self-care, self-compassion, and self-awareness.

Your inner champion is your inner compass, guiding you through life's challenges.Unleashing your inner champion creates a ripple effect, inspiring others to do the same.You are the architect of your destiny. Unleash your inner champion and build a life of purpose.

Chapter 14(Maintaining momentum:overcoming obstacles and staying focused)

Maintaining momentum requires relentless drive and resilience. Winners anticipate obstacles and adapt strategies.Life's challenges can either stall or propel you forward. Your inner champion chooses the latter.Every setback contains a lesson. Winners learn, adjust, and surge forward.

Momentum builders include celebrating small wins, setting achievable goals, and surrounding yourself with positive influences.Self-care and self-compassion fuel your inner champion. Prioritize physical and mental well-being.Resilience is key to maintaining momentum. Develop coping strategies and bounce back stronger.

Focus on progress, not perfection. Winners celebrate milestones and stay committed.Your inner champion thrives on challenges. Embrace difficulties as growth opportunities.Maintaining momentum demands flexibility. Adapt, innovate, and stay ahead.

Winners prioritize accountability. Surround yourself with people who fuel your inner champion.Your legacy depends on maintaining momentum. Leave a lasting impact.Unstoppable winners maintain momentum through continuous learning and self-improvement.Stay focused, stay driven, and your inner champion will propel you to greatness.

Momentum is contagious. Share your success with others and inspire a wave of achievement.Winners recognize momentum killers: procrastination, self-doubt, and fear. Confront and overcome them.Your inner champion fuels momentum. Nurture it with positive self-talk and affirmations.Setbacks are temporary. Maintain momentum by focusing on long-term goals.

Resilience is built through adversity. Embrace challenges as strength-building opportunities.Celebrate milestones, no matter how small. Momentum grows with acknowledgment.Your environment impacts momentum. Surround yourself with positivity and productivity.Maintaining momentum requires balance. Prioritize self-care and well-being.

Focus on progress, not perfection. Momentum thrives on continuous improvement.Winners adjust strategies to maintain momentum. Stay adaptable and innovative.Momentum is a mindset. Choose to maintain it, and your inner champion will propel you forward.

Invest in continuous learning to fuel momentum. Knowledge is power.Surround yourself with momentum builders: supportive people, inspiring books, and empowering experiences.Your inner champion is your momentum catalyst. Trust it, and unstoppable success follows.Maintaining momentum creates a ripple effect, inspiring others to achieve greatness.

Momentum ignites passion, driving you toward greatness. Fan the flames with meaningful goals.Your inner champion fuels momentum's fire. Nurture it with self-care and positivity.Resilience is momentum's backbone. Develop coping strategies to overcome obstacles.

Momentum builders include accountability partners, progress tracking, and celebration.Maintaining momentum demands flexibility. Adapt to changes and innovate.

Your environment shapes momentum. Surround yourself with inspiring people and places.Focus on the journey, not just the destination. Momentum lies in progress.Winners prioritize momentum over mediocrity. Choose excellence.Momentum grows with gratitude. Acknowledge progress and appreciate support.

Invest in continuous learning to propel momentum. Knowledge fuels growth.Surround yourself with momentum accelerators: inspiring stories, empowering quotes, and motivational music.Your inner champion is momentum's spark. Trust it, and unstoppable success follows.Momentum creates a success snowball effect. Small wins fuel larger achievements.

Maintaining momentum requires self-awareness. Recognize and overcome self-limiting beliefs.Winners maintain momentum through continuous improvement. Strive for excellence.Momentum fuels confidence, resilience, and determination. Unlock your inner champion.

16

Chapter 15(Leaving a lasting legacy: The ultimate measure of success)

A lasting legacy is the ultimate measure of success. Winners leave an indelible mark.Your legacy is shaped by daily choices. Choose wisely.Impact is not limited to grand gestures. Small actions can leave lasting impressions.

Legacy builders include mentorship, community service, and inspiring others.Your inner champion fuels legacy. Nurture it with purpose and passion.A lasting legacy requires resilience. Overcome obstacles and stay committed.

Legacy is not solely individual. Collaborate, empower, and uplift others.Your story has the power to inspire. Share it.Legacy extends beyond your lifetime. Consider the impact on future generations.Winners prioritize legacy over personal gain. Leave a lasting difference.

Self-awareness and selflessness shape legacy. Understand your purpose.Your values and principles form legacy's foundation.

Stand firm.A lasting legacy demands continuous learning. Stay informed, adapt, and innovate.Invest in people, not just projects. Empower others to carry forward your legacy.Your legacy is your immortality. Leave a lasting impact.

Legacy is a reflection of your values, principles, and passions. Ensure alignment.Inspiring others is a powerful legacy builder. Share your story.Collaboration and empowerment create lasting impact. Build a legacy team.Your legacy benefits from continuous improvement. Stay curious.Invest in the next generation. Mentorship fuels lasting legacy.Selflessness shapes legacy. Prioritize the greater good.Resilience ensures legacy endures. Overcome obstacles.

Authenticity is crucial to legacy. Stay true to yourself.Legacy extends beyond accomplishments. Leave a lasting impression.Your inner champion fuels legacy. Nurture it.Legacy requires intentional effort. Prioritize.A lasting legacy transforms lives. Strive for significance.Your legacy story will outlive you. Make it inspiring.Legacy is a reflection of your character, values, and impact. Ensure it inspires.Your story has the power to transform lives. Share it boldly.Investing in others' growth creates lasting legacy. Empower and mentor.

Resilience in adversity strengthens legacy. Persevere with purpose.Authenticity and integrity form legacy's foundation. Stand firm.Collaboration and teamwork amplify legacy. Build a united front.Selflessness and generosity expand legacy's reach. Give freely.Continuous learning and growth fuel legacy. Stay curious.

Legacy extends beyond accomplishments. Leave a lasting impression.Your inner champion drives legacy. Nurture and trust it.Intentional effort shapes lasting legacy. Prioritize and focus.Legacy transforms lives and inspires generations. Strive for significance.

Your legacy story will outlive you. Make it unforgettable.Legacy is not solely individual. Family, community, and society benefit.Empowering others empowers legacy. Create a ripple effect.Legacy requires courage, resilience, and determination. Stay committed.Inspiring others inspires legacy. Share your passion and purpose.Legacy is a lifelong journey. Stay focused, stay driven.

17

Recap

Introduction

- Introduced the concept of the winner's mindset
    - Emphasized the importance of cultivating a winning mindset for success

Key Principles

1. Self-Awareness: Understanding your strengths, weaknesses, and purpose
2. Resilience: Overcoming obstacles and setbacks
3. Focus: Maintaining a clear vision and priorities
4. Courage: Embracing challenges and taking calculated risks
5. Authenticity: Staying true to yourself and your values
6. Growth Mindset: Continuously learning and improving
7. Positive Self-Talk: Nurturing a supportive inner voice
8. Accountability: Surrounding yourself with supportive people

Unleashing Your Inner Champion

1. Identifying and overcoming self-limiting beliefs
2. Building confidence and self-trust
3. Embracing vulnerability and authenticity
4. Developing emotional intelligence

Maintaining Momentum

1. Setting achievable goals and celebrating progress
2. Prioritizing self-care and well-being
3. Surrounding yourself with positive influences
4. Embracing challenges as growth opportunities

Leaving a Lasting Legacy

1. Defining your purpose and values
2. Building meaningful relationships
3. Inspiring and empowering others
4. Leaving a lasting impact

Conclusion

- Recap of key takeaways
    - Encouragement to apply the principles

- Inspiration to unleash your inner champion

Key Takeaways

- Cultivate self-awareness, resilience, and focus
    - Embrace challenges and growth opportunities
    - Stay authentic, positive, and accountable
    - Unleash your inner champion
    - Leave a lasting legacy

18

Call to action

Take the First Step Towards Unleashing Your Inner Champion

Now that you've discovered the secrets to cultivating a winner's mindset, it's time to put them into action.

Join the Winner's Circle:

1. Visit our website: [https://www.facebook.com/profile.php?id=61566550829757&mibextid=LQQJ4d]

Take the 30-Day Winner's Challenge:

1. Commit to daily self-reflection and growth
2. Apply one new principle each day
3. Share your progress with our community

Unlock Exclusive Content:

1. Get access to expert interviews and webinars
2. Receive personalized coaching and guidance
3. Join our private Winner's Circle community

Invest in Yourself:

1. Schedule a coaching session: [insert coaching URL]
2. Enroll in our online course: [insert course URL]
3. Attend a live event: [insert event URL]

Share Your Story:

1. Write a review on Amazon/Goodreads
2. Share your testimonial on social media
3. Inspire others with your winning mindset

Remember:

You have the power to unleash your inner champion.

You have the potential to achieve greatness.

Take the first step today.

Start Your Winning Journey Now!

[Insert Call-to-Action button: Join Now, Get Started, etc.]

This call to action:

1. Encourages readers to engage with the content
2. Offers exclusive resources and support
3. Invites readers to join a community
4. Provides opportunities for growth and development
5. Inspires readers to take action

19

Inspirational note

"You are stronger than you think.

You are braver than you feel.

And you are capable of achieving greatness.

Believe in yourself.

Trust your instincts.

And never give up on your dreams.

You have a unique purpose.

A distinct voice.

And a profound impact to make.

Unleash your inner champion.

Embrace your true potential.

The world needs your light.

Your love.

And your unwavering resilience.

Rise above obstacles.

Shine through challenges.

And remember:

Every setback is an opportunity.

Every failure is a lesson.

And every success is a testament to your strength.

You are unstoppable.

Keep shining.

Keep pushing.

And keep believing.

In yourself.

And your incredible potential."

"Your journey is unique.

Your path is yours alone.

Don't compare.

Don't doubt.

Trust the process.

Trust yourself.

Every step forward.

Every leap of faith.

Leads you closer.

To your dreams.

Your aspirations.

And your true greatness.

Keep moving.

Keep striving.

And know:

You are enough.

You are worthy.

And you are loved."

20

Final thoughts

As you close this book, remember that your journey to greatness has just begun. You've unlocked the secrets to unleashing your inner champion, and now it's time to apply them. Embrace challenges with courage, transform obstacles into opportunities, and turn your vision into reality. Your winning mindset is your greatest asset; nurture it, protect it, and unleash its full potential. Believe in yourself, own your strengths, and live your dreams. Your legacy awaits, so leave a lasting impact, inspire others, and change the world. Stay focused, driven, and committed to your aspirations, and remember that you are strong, resilient, capable, and unstoppable. May your journey be bright, your heart be bold, and your spirit remain unbroken.Your winning journey starts today; embrace the mindset, unleash the champion, and change the world. You've discovered the power within; now harness it. Stay true to yourself, your values, and your purpose. Overcome obstacles, learn from setbacks, and rise above limitations. Your inner champion will guide you; trust it. Inspire others with your story, your passion, and your success. Leave a lasting legacy that transcends time. You are unstoppable; keep shining, keep pushing, and keep believing in yourself and your incredible potential.

Your journey to greatness is unique, and so is your path. Don't compare; focus on your progress. Celebrate small wins, learn from setbacks, and stay committed.You've grown, you've learned, and you've transformed.   Now, share your story. Inspire others with your resilience, your courage, and your determination.

The winner's mindset is not a destination; it's a journey. Stay humble, stay hungry, and stay open to growth. Continuously learn, adapt, and evolve.Your inner champion is your greatest ally. Trust it, nurture it, and unleash its full potential. You are capable of achieving greatness; believe it.

As you embark on your winning journey, remember that obstacles are opportunities. Challenges are stepping stones. And setbacks are lessons.You are stronger than you think, braver than you feel, and more resilient than you know. Keep pushing, keep striving, and keep believing.

Your legacy is not just what you leave behind; it's what you build every day. Focus on the present, stay committed to your vision, and inspire others.The power to achieve greatness lies within you. Unleash it, harness it, and share it with the world.Stay focused, stay driven, and stay committed to your dreams. Your winning journey starts today.

21

About the author

Tshireletso Prince Phaahle is a visionary author and inspirational thought leader born in September 2003. With a profound understanding of human potential and a passion for empowering others, Prince has dedicated his life to helping individuals unlock their inner strength and achieve greatness. Through his writing, he shares insightful wisdom, garnered from his experiences and studies, to inspire a new generation of leaders and change-makers. Prince's remarkable perspective, creativity, and generosity of spirit shine through in his debut book, "The Winner's Mindset," a testament to his commitment to transforming lives and leaving a lasting impact.

Meet Tshireletso Prince Phaahle, a talented young author born in September 2003, with a burning desire to inspire and uplift others. Prince's writing embodies his enthusiasm, empathy, and understanding of the human experience. In "The Winner's Mindset," he generously shares his insights and expertise, guiding readers on a transformative journey of self-discovery and growth. With his bright mind and compassionate heart, Prince is poised to become a leading voice in personal development and motivational literature.

Author:Tshireletso Prince Phaahle

Email:phaahleprince9@icloud.com/phaahleprince9@gmail.com

Contact:0662312576

facebook page:https://www.facebook.com/profile.php?id=61566550829757&mibextid=LQQJ4d

Amazon page:[https://www.amazon.com/author/phaahleprince.amazon.com]

Founder of Tshireparadise book club

22

Final message

Final Message

"Thank you for joining me on this transformative journey. May the principles of 'The Winner's Mindset' guide you towards greatness.

Remember, your story is unique, and your impact is awaited.

Stay unstoppable.

"Congratulations on taking the first step towards unleashing your inner champion!

Keep shining, keep pushing, and keep believing.

The world needs your light.

"As you close this book, remember: your winning journey has just begun.

Stay focused, stay driven, and stay committed.

Unleash your greatness.

"You've reached the end of this book, but the beginning of your winning journey.

Empower others, inspire change, and leave a lasting legacy.

Thank you for being part of this movement.
— Tshireletso Prince Phaahle"

I LOVE YOU ALL!!

"May God's peace guide you, His strength empower you, and His love surround you on your winning journey." - Philippians 4:13

"Remember, you are fearfully and wonderfully made. Unleash your greatness for His glory." - Psalm 139:14

"May the Lord bless you and keep you, make His face shine upon you, and give you peace." - Numbers 6:24-26

"Walk by faith, not by sight. Trust in the Lord with all your heart." - 2 Corinthians 5:7, Proverbs 3:5

"May God's Word be a lamp unto your feet, guiding you towards greatness." - Psalm 119:105

"You are the light of the world. Shine bright, and let your light inspire others." - Matthew 5:14-16

"May the grace of the Lord Jesus Christ be with you always." - 2 Corinthians 13:14

"For I know the plans I have for you," declares the Lord, "plans to prosper you and not to harm you, plans to give you hope and a future." - Jeremiah 29:11

Printed in Dunstable, United Kingdom